Especially 4 Me
A Student's Guide To Understanding The IEP

Angelise M. Rouse, Ph.D.

www.Especially4MePublishing.com

Cheers for the IEP Made Easy...

"This book is an easy read for a student through the eyes of a student. It has the ability to draw in a youngster and captivate their interest so that they can understand the process much better and become an active participant and self-advocate for their education. This is a great resource for all children once they become of age for self-advocacy. I would recommend this book."
Devon J. Russaw
Assistant Principal,
Former Special Education Teacher

"Kudos to Dr. Rouse for writing **Especially 4 Me.** *This is a good introduction into the IEP landscape and the daily operation of Special Education services. Dr. Rouse highlights in the text important issues that are currently affecting young people with learning disabilities. This is a scenario based book which gives insight to helping students with exceptionalities cope with the challenges they face."*
Dr. Brita A. Theadford
Supervisor of Curriculum and Instruction

"Dr. Rouse is an exceptional, empathetic, nurturing educator who I had the pleasure of co-teaching with. It is no surprise to me that Angelise took the time to write this manual so students could be equipped with the knowledge they need to ensure and be accountable for their success. Dr. Angelis Rouse... Kudos!!! Continue advocating for young people and empowering them with knowledge."
Shirreca Bradham
Language Arts Instructor

"Dr. Rouse has written a simplistic guide for students, empowering them to become an active part in the IEP process. This short thorough guide will assist students in self-advocacy. The dialogue is written and shared through the eyes of a student. This is a powerful message to other student-peers."
Tamera Foley, Ph.D.

*"**Especially 4 Me: A Student's Guide to Understanding the IEP**, is a welcome resource for students and parents navigating through Special Education. This engaging resource told by a student and his peers, empowers and motivates students to seriously think about their future after high school."*
Dr. Natasha Veale
Associate Professor of Special Education,
Greensboro College

"There is no time like the present! Dr. Rouse has written a student-narrated guide to the IEP process that explains the necessary steps in entering a Special Education Program through high school, with a focus on student transition and self-advocacy for their future. **Especially 4 Me** *is a much needed resource for students, parents, and school districts."*
Dr. Edris Ryan
Educational Expert, College Professor and
Special Education Consultant
CEC Member

Copyright 2015 by Angelise M. Rouse, Ph.D. All Rights Reserved.

No part of this book may be reproduced or transmitted in any form or by any means, electronic or mechanical, including photocopying and recording, or by any information storage and retrieval system, without permission in writing from authors and publisher.

Printed in the United States of America
2015 First Edition
10 9 8 7 6 5 4 3 2 1

Cover & Interior Design: Nick Macedo, FirmZero.com
Author Photo Credit: Greg White Sr.

Subject Index:
Rouse, Angelise M.
Title: Especially 4 Me: A Student's Guide to Understanding the IEP
1. Special Education
2. IDEA
3. IEP
4. Transition & Advocacy

Paperback ISBN: 978-0-69255525-5

Especially 4 Me Publishing LLC
www.especially4me.com
drangeliserouse@especially4me.com

To all of the students who
have enriched my life.

No matter what, always know
that you are truly special.

TABLE OF CONTENTS

INTRODUCTION	11
Meet Drew Matthews	14
The IEP Referral	16
CHAPTER ONE: A FRESH START - DREW'S HOUSE	17
What is Special Education?	22
What is an IEP	23
What is No Child Left Behind?	25
What is IDEA	26
Least Restrictive Environment (LRE)	27
Celebrities with Disabilities	29
The 504 Plan	32
CHAPTER TWO: THE RIGHT MOVES - HIGH SCHOOL	33
What Types of IEP Meetings Are There?	34
Self-Advocacy	39
CHAPTER THREE: A GIANT STEP FORWARD - Drew's School Cafeteria	45
What Are Transition Services?	50
What Goals & Strategies Should Be Included in Your Transition Plan?	51

Appendices	55
Appendix A	56
Appendix B	57
Appendix C	58
Appendix D	59
Appendix E	60
Appendix F	61
Appendix G	68
Appendix H	70
Appendix I	73
About the Author	77
Contact	79
Notebook	80

INTRODUCTION

"Develop a passion for learning. If you do, you will never cease to grow."
ANTHONY J. D'ANGELO

I have attended hundreds of Individual Education Plan ("IEP") meetings, seminars, and continuing education courses in Special Education. However, it's the IEP meeting that has constantly given me pause. Each time I walk out of an IEP meeting, I feel a tightening in my gut as I recall the confusion, fear, and uncertainty on a student's face when his parent, teachers, and other professionals, discuss his educational future. My constant visual takeaway of *"What just happened?"* is my primary reason for writing this short story. I hope this story paints a clearer picture of the IEP process for you, the student.

As you read this handbook, you will learn many new and important facts related to students in Special Education. It is important for you to get a snapshot of what the future holds once your new IEP has been developed, signed and implemented. It is my hope that you attend college or begin a career of your choice regardless of any learning challenges you may have.

Time and again, I try to put myself in your shoes to imagine being a teenager, while the adults in the room use several acronyms and advanced vocabulary to make decisions about my future. I've seen most teens just tune out, and leave all of the decision-making to the adults. As you read this story, make a decision to take the next phase of your life and career planning seriously. Take an active role in planning your education. Be confident, ask questions and succeed.

Understanding and keeping abreast of the Special Education laws is a huge task for professionals like me in the field. I often find myself reviewing the lengthy federal and state laws that govern the teacher instruction for the millions of students with disabilities in the United States. There are mandatory yearly reviews, a lot of paperwork, follow up, and professionals involved in this very important process. However, with the help of educators and parents, as well as available federal and state services, you can achieve great success. If you want more details about Special Education see the Appendices at the end of this handbook.

This simple story is designed with you in mind, so that you will understand the IEP process from one of your peers, Drew Matthews, and a few of his friends. The main goal is to empower you to take a more active role in your academic future in high school. Life is about choices. The sooner you make intentional and positive choices, the better positioned you will be to succeed in life. This book was designed Especially 4 You!

- Dr. Angelise M. Rouse

"Obstacles don't have to stop you. If you run into a wall, don't turn around and give up. Figure out how to climb it, go through it, or work around it."
MICHAEL JORDAN

MEET
DREW MATTHEWS

AGE: 15

GRADE: FINISHING LAST QUARTER OF 9TH GRADE

DREW'S FAVORITES:

THINGS TO DO: DRAWING, COMPUTER GRAPHICS, & PLAY NBA 2K

SPORT: BASKETBALL

PLAYER: LEBRON JAMES

FOOD: PIZZA

RESTAURANT: FRIDAY'S

SINGER: DRAKE

CAREER GOAL: GRAPHICS DESIGNER
MOVIE SET DESIGNER

"I went through an assessment and referral process in elementary school that qualified me to receive Special Education services because of my unique disability. All kids in public school Special Education must go through an assessment or evaluation to determine their academic capabilities."

THE
REFERRAL PROCESS

Referral Made by anyone involved with the child's education and development, including the parents, teacher, principal, pediatrician, or Child Study Team (CST) Member

Evaluation by psychologist and other education professionals

Qualified for Special Education Services

IEP Placement

Annual Review

Re-Evaluation Every 3 Years

CHAPTER ONE
A FRESH START
DREW'S HOUSE

Depending on a student's disability, they will be placed in one of three types of classes:
i) Inclusive: regular education class with your peers along with a special education teacher
ii) Resource: classes with a Special Education teacher in small groups based on what subjects you need help with; and
iii) Self-contained: all of your classes in the same room with a Special Education teacher and usually a paraprofessional.

When I woke up this morning I felt strange. Different, but in a cool way. I grabbed my phone from under my pillow. What? It's 6:00 AM! I don't think I've ever been up this early for school. *Is today a school day?* I said to myself. Should I pretend to go back to sleep until mom comes in at 7:00? Every morning she bangs on the door and then just walks right in. No words. She pulls off my covers and walks out.

Is this a dream? Have I been kidnapped by real zombies? Is this the apocalypse? I decided to just roll with the morning, shower, and be ready before mom knocked on the door. Besides, the shock on her face when she sees me dressed will be worth it.

Just as I stood up my phone vibrated. I checked it. Jeff texted me. Now this is definitely straight up crazy. Jeff is late for school every day, and I am usually right behind him. How can he be up now? I called him.

Drew: Why you up this early?

Jeff: Drew, I didn't know how early it really was, but my pops is tired of me being late all the time, so this morning he said I need to be out by 6:30 or else!"

Drew: For real?

Jeff: No joke. So I'll be over by you in a few.

Drew: Cool.

Chapter One: Fresh Start – Drew's House

I dropped the phone on the bed and walked toward the bathroom and the phone rang. It was Shayna. This is even more weird than Jeff coming over. Shayna has never called me in the morning. We usually meet up at lunch and kick it for the rest of the day.

Drew: Hello.

Shayna: Hey Drew, just wanted to remind you of what day it is.

Drew: What? Why are you calling me in the morning?

Shayna: I wanted to remind you of your IEP meeting today.

Drew: Oh wow. I wasn't sure why I was feeling strange this morning.

Shayna: What do you mean?

Drew: Well, first I woke up at 6 o'clock with a smile on my face. Then Jeff called and said his pops is kicking him out at 6:30, so he's headed over. Now, you call me in the morning which you have never done, to tell me about my IEP meeting.

Shayna: As your best friend, I just didn't want you to get to school and be surprised because your mom and my mom are carpooling today. The meeting starts first period.

Drew: It did slip my mind when I woke up but now I remember. Today I get to pick my classes for tenth grade. I really hope I can get into the Graphics Design class. Shayna, I've got to jump in the shower before Jeff gets here.

Shayna: OK see you later.

I left the front door open so Jeff didn't wake up my little brother. Mom was already up because I heard Channel Six news on her TV. When Jeff got here I was already dressed.

Jeff: What's the occasion? You going to a party this early?

Drew: No man. I have my annual IEP meeting. My mom always says I have to look presentable, so I put on this button-down shirt and khakis.

Jeff: You know, all this time we've been boys, you never talked about your IEP. When I first heard you and Shayna talking about it a while ago, I thought you were talking about a special at IHOP!

Drew: Man, you're crazy!

Jeff: Drew, I knew you were in Special Ed., but you've always been cool with me, so that doesn't matter.

Drew: Thanks Jeff. Most kids in Special Ed. have some type of disability, but it doesn't mean we are stupid. We just learn differently. Most of us were evaluated by some type of specialist when we were younger and they found something unique about the way we learn.

Jeff: Oh I get it. As long as I've known you Drew, you are definitely not stupid! So what does the IEP mean anyway? If you don't tell me, I'll just Google it!

Drew: Like I said, man, you're crazy!

Jeff: So Drew, is this Special Education thing really a big deal?

Drew: Are you kidding? Yes, it's a big deal to both the state where we live and the federal government. Did you know that the law guarantees unique rights to people with disabilities?

Jeff: No. I didn't know that.

Drew: Then just Google it!

Jeff: I'll take your word for it now and Google it later.

WHAT IS SPECIAL EDUCATION?

Special education is specially designed instruction, support, and services program provided to students in public schools with an identified disability. It requires individually designed instructional programs to meet our unique learning needs. The purpose of special education is to enable students to successfully develop to their fullest potential. All of the rules for Special Education must be in compliance with the Individuals with Disabilities Education Act (IDEA). Federal and state services are provided to students in special education until they are 21 years old.

WHAT IS AN IEP?

An IEP is an Individualized Education Plan developed for students with disabilities to ensure their educational goals are achieved. An IEP is a required step in the process of receiving Special Education services. A student's parents, teachers, and other service providers meet to come to agreement about the educational accommodations necessary to assist the student(s) in meeting the objectives.

The IEP has a lot of pages and details about your learning abilities. It is broken down into different sections and lays out the types of SpecialEducation services you should receive: 1) Present level of performance based on your tests and other evaluations, 2) Special accommodations, 3) Goals for the year, 4) Special services you need and 5) The transition. Every year there is a reevaluation of all parts.

WHAT IS NO CHILD LEFT BEHIND?

No Child Left Behind Act- 2001 (NCLB) - This is a federal law that applies to general education students and students with disabilities in public schools. All states must administer assessments to all students. It requires schools to closely monitor student's academic achievements so that they can make Adequate Yearly Progress (**AYP**) to move to the next grade. If students fail to make AYP, then the schools could face penalties. Students are assessed based on their grade and subject matter.

WHAT IS IDEA?

Individuals with Disabilities Education Improvement Act - 2004 (IDEA) is a federal law that gives specific educational services to kids in Special Education from Pre K through high school. IDEA makes it possible for Special Education students to have an IEP. All students in Special Education are classified based on their disability which can be mental or physical. Eligible students with disabilities are entitled to a **"free appropriate public education" (FAPE).** FAPE requires public schools to provide students with an education, including specialized instruction and related services that prepares the child for further education, employment, and independent living.

LRE

IDEA also requires that students be placed in the Least Restrictive Environment (LRE) so they can succeed with support. IDEA has several categories for disabilities which can be found in the Appendix. LRE is an important concept for students, parents and educators to understand. The LRE section guarantees a student's right to be educated in a setting like his or her peers without disabilities. This gives students an even greater chance of success with the right support, accommodations and curriculum modifications.

Drew: Kids in Special Education are not stupid. We just learn differently. I'm not going to let my disability hold me back from becoming a graphics designer.

Jeff: Now that's what's up Drew! Remember when we were in class and Mr. Wilson pulled up that website that listed celebrities with disabilities?

Drew: Oh, I remember. There are so many successful business people and celebrities that were in a Special Education Program.

CELEBRITIES WITH DISABILITIES

- Daymond John - FUBU Founder, businessman, and Shark Tank.

- Tommy Hilfiger - Fashion Designer

- Steven Spielberg - Movie Writer/Director

- Justin Timberlake - Singer

- Tim Tebow - NFL Quarterback

- Daniel Radcliffe - Actor (Harry Potter)

- Keira Knightley - Actress (Pirates of the Caribbean)

Jeff: No way man! That Harry Potter dude has a disability? Justin Timberlake? Wow. That's unbelievable!

Drew: Like I said. I'm not going to let my disability stop me from reaching my dreams like all of them. Jeff, if we leave now, we can catch the 7:30 bus.

Jeff: Cool.

Drew: Mom, I'm out. Jeff and I can make the bus.

Mom: I can't believe it! I don't think I've ever heard those words before. See you at the meeting.

For the first time since I can remember, I left the house to go to school and my mom did not wake me up. It feels good being responsible. I'm going to convince Jeff that we need to make a pact to be on time for school starting now.

Did you know that students who are gifted and talented can also receive Special Education services? You know the type of kids who are smarter than everyone (even the teacher) in certain subjects, athletic abilities, creative abilities, and excel in visual or performing arts? Like I said, we are not stupid, we just learn differently. You shouldn't let your disability stop you from reaching your dreams.

THE
504 PLAN

Federal Rehabilitation Act to Prohibit Public School Discrimination Based on a disability)

Student does not qualify for Special Education IEP Plan

Provides specific student accommodations and support services

Student likely in general education classes

No annual goals like IEP

Same type of Child Study Team professionals and parent involvement

CHAPTER TWO
THE RIGHT MOVES
HIGH SCHOOL

Jeff and I arrived so early that they were still serving breakfast. Neither of us had ever been to school this early. It was weird because it was a lot quieter than we were used to.

Drew: I guess we should see what they have for breakfast since we're here.

Jeff: Breakfast? Man Drew we never eat in the morning!

Drew: Well I think we should start today. Remember I have my IEP meeting to pick my classes for tenth grade. I need to start feeding my brain in the morning. I think you should too.

Jeff and I had pancakes. It wasn't bad for school lunch. Who knows? Maybe I should try to get to school earlier just for the breakfast! The bell rang. Jeff went to his homeroom. He was in the same homeroom as Shayna. My homeroom was on a different floor. Everyone started piling into class. A few kids snapped on my pink button-down shirt. That didn't bother me. I knew it was a really a cool shirt even though it was pink.

WHAT TYPES OF IEP MEETINGS ARE THERE?

- The first one is called the "Initial" meeting

- Then there is an "Annual Review" of the decisions made in a previous year's meeting; and then

- There is a "Reevaluation," which happens every three years. This meeting can be held whenever there is a concern that the student's IEP is no longer meeting his or her needs.

The bell rang again. It was time for first period. Today I was excused from my early morning classes because I had my IEP meeting. The meeting was in Ms. Pearson's office, my Case Manager. I always liked Ms. Pearson because she reminded me of my mom—straight to the point and never let me get away with slacking off.

The door was open so I walked in. Four adults were already seated around Ms. Pearson's desk. *Why are all these people here and up so early?* I said to myself.

This is the Child Study Team (CST) that showed up for my IEP meeting:
Ms. Pearson - Learning Disability Teacher Consultant (LDTC) and Case Manager,
Ms. Hamilton - Special Education Teacher,
Mr. Lloyd - History Teacher,
Ms. Walden - Guidance Counselor,
me & my mom.

As part of the IEP meeting, make sure you write down the things that you are good at doing, and things that you are interested in learning about. Also write down things that you don't like to do. What do you think your future career will be? The more you think about it beforehand, the better off you will be.

Ms. Walden: Good morning Drew. We've been waiting for you. Go ahead and take a seat next to your mom.

Drew: OK.

Ms. Walden: Now we have a lot to cover this morning so I'm going ask everyone present to sign in on the document that I pass around. After that, I will turn things over to Ms. Pearson to explain the purpose and of goals of Drew's IEP meeting.

Ms. Pearson: The primary purpose of this meeting is to review Drew's current IEP which includes his current academic program, modifications, accommodations, and current educational goals and objectives. This yearly review allows the IEP Team to revisit the terms of his current IEP, to determine whether it is meeting Drew's individual needs and to assess whether he is making adequate progress toward annual goals. We will revise the IEP for the coming school year, and consider next year's IEP goals. Drew, do you know what all of this means?

Drew: Sort of.

Ms. Walden: That's fine. The most important thing is that when you leave here today you will have a better understanding of your educational goals for the upcoming school year.

SELF-ADVOCACY

The ability to self-advocate is important for you to learn in order to be successful at all stages of your life. Self-advocacy is when you can understand and effectively communicate your needs to other people; things like your strengths, weaknesses, your likes and dislikes.

Ms. Pearson: Now I'd like to turn things over to your Special Education teacher, Ms. Hamilton.

Ms. Hamilton: Drew, let's talk about your plans for after graduation. Tell us a few of your interests. What are some things you like to do?

Drew's Mom: He's very good at drawing. He wants to be a graphics designer.

Drew: Ever since I was little I've wanted to make money drawing my ideas.

Ms. Hamilton: I agree Drew, you are a very good artist as I have seen a lot of your work in class.

Ms. Pearson handed out a package of papers to everyone. She started reading out loud my Present Level Performance (PLP) from my teachers. I looked over at my mom and she smiled. I was right on target with meeting my goals. I'm glad to have friends like Jeff and Shayna to help me with my school work as well. The three of us are on a path to success.

Ms. Walden: I started working on this class schedule for you Drew. There are several courses available to you. I wanted to make sure you got into the intro graphic design class. As you see, you must take English 2, Science, Math, Physical Education/Health and another history course. You can choose one more elective since you already have Graphics Design 1.

Drew: I was nervous about getting into the Graphics design class because I heard so many kids saying they wanted to take it. Plus I heard it was a tough class.

Ms. Pearson: Well there is no need to worry. This class will have a paraprofessional or teacher in the classroom with the regular teacher to modify and adapt lesson plans. She is there to provide you extra support and accommodations as outlined in your IEP.

Mr. Lloyd: So it looks like all of the academics are in order. The special education teacher and I will make sure you get support and extra help in your history class. No worries!

Drew: Thanks.

Drew's Mom: Is there another writing course he can take? I'd like to see a writing course on his schedule. I think he needs to work on his writing since he has so many great ideas. He must be able to express them on paper.

Ms. Pearson: You're right, written expression is an important part of communication. For students, developing strong writing skills not only helps their grades but also prepares them for their academic and professional futures. All of our students are expected to graduate high school with effective written and verbal language skills. I am sure that his teacher can supply supplemental materials for him. We can discuss this further with his teacher.

By third period we were all still in the IEP meeting. I felt good about this part of the process. For the first time I saw myself closer to my dream of being a graphic designer. I couldn't wait to meet up with Jeff and Shayna at lunch to tell them more about it. I'm so glad that we were all now in the same high school.

Most parents and students don't know that if they have questions or want to change something in the IEP, they can do it during the school year and they don't have to wait for the annual IEP reevaluation meeting. Both you and your parents have a lot of rights regarding your IEP so make sure you know them or be sure to ask your Special Education teacher.

CHAPTER THREE
A GIANT STEP FORWARD
DREW'S HIGH SCHOOL CAFETERIA

My IEP meeting went very good. I remember feeling nervous about going to high school at the beginning of the year. It was really a big deal. At first, I was worried about whether the other kids thought I was normal or if the older kids would tease me for being in Special Education. I'm half way through the finish line, so I really don't worry about that anymore. I know that I'm special in my own way. I know that I can do things that a lot of other kids can't do.

I know that if I work hard, I can graduate and start graphic design school. Not only am I happy with myself, my mom is also happy. I feel like we've both come a long way since my referral from my second grade teacher. Drew was finally growing up and I have my mom to thank. She never missed an IEP meeting or an opportunity to speak with my teachers and case managers. Your parents should be actively involved in your IEP.

There was only five minutes to spare before it was time for fourth period. I was so psyched about the meeting. I couldn't wait to get to lunch to tell Jeff and Shayna about my classes. Shayna would be the most excited because she wants to be a Special Education teacher like her mom. The bell rang. It was finally lunch time. Jeff, Shayna and I met at the same lunch table in the corner. I arrived first, so I got my lunch and headed to our table. They both joined me a little while later.

Jeff: Hey Drew, pink is really your color!

Drew: Whatever man!

Shayna: OK so tell me, did you get the graphics design course?

Drew: Yes! It was the only course I was worried about. Everything else was fine.

Shayna: I'm so happy for you! I can't wait to see the cool stuff you create.

Jeff: Me neither.

Drew: Just think, in a few months we will be heading to the tenth grade.

Shayna: I know. Things are happening very fast. Remember when we were younger and you used to beg both of our mom's to put us in the same class?

Drew: I can't believe you remember that.

Shayna: How could I ever forget you running down the halls and barging into my class!

Jeff: He really did that?

Shayna: A few times a month until we were in fourth grade and then we had two classes together; English and Art.

Drew: I just felt so out of place and different from the other kids. Some kids called me a dummy because I stayed in the same class all day. I knew Shayna was smart and I wanted to be in the smart class like her. I worked really hard, even in the summer and before I knew it, I was taking some inclusion classes with the general ed students.

Shayna: Yes Art was so much fun. Drew always won prizes for his artwork.

Jeff: I know. He is one of the best I've ever seen.

Drew: This feels like we're getting old. Talking about the good old days of elementary school. Just think, we survived middle school, and now we are almost half way through high school. Besides, Ms. Walden and I have already started working on my transitional plan. Now that's what's up!

Shayna: Like I said, things are happening very fast so we all need to get our acts together.

Jeff: Drew and I already made a pact to eat breakfast and get to school on time. That's a major change for both of us.

Shayna: Yes, that is major for you guys! I hope you stick with it.

Chapter Three: A Giant Step Forward – Drew's School Cafeteria

School attendance is important. Come to school even when you don't feel like it. Teachers don't always feel like coming to school either, but they do it because they know that it is important and want to help you succeed. Be on time and be prepared. It can only help as you transition into your future career goals.

WHAT ARE TRANSITION SERVICES?

Many states provide for transition in two phases. The first phase is when the student reaches age 14 and is entering high school. The other phase is when the student is 16 and is near completion of high school. At this age, the student will work with Special Education professionals to prepare, identify, and develop goals which need to be accomplished during the current school year to assist the student in meeting his post-high school goals.

Transition services help prepare students for life after high school. The plan at age 16 should include measurable goals towards graduation and higher education, whether vocational school or a job.
The more involvement you have in the transition process, the better your chances of receiving the services and support you need to reach your goals.

WHAT GOALS & STRATEGIES SHOULD BE INCLUDED IN YOUR TRANSITION PLAN?

- College bound: Better study skills, work with teachers to ensure you meet all requirements for college admission, and research colleges and universities with accommodations for students with learning disabilities.

- Job bound: Resume writing, reading job search ads, completing job applications, life skills and customer service skills.

Even though Jeff, Shayna and I are young, we have all given serious thought to our future careers. Shayna has pretended to be a teacher since we were little. She is very smart, kind, and has a lot of patience. I know she will be a great teacher one day. Jeff wants to be a sports agent. I think he will be good at it because he knows a lot about all sports and is always talking to get the last word. He is a great negotiator– even his teachers think so.

Chapter Three: A Giant Step Forward – Drew's School Cafeteria

Being in Special Education and having an IEP follow you from elementary school throughout high school is not such a bad thing. It can only help you get the individualized education to meet your needs based on your disability. Ask your parents and your teachers a lot of questions so you have a good understanding of each step of your IEP process. Your future is very special and it's in your hands.

FOR MORE INFORMATION ABOUT THE IEP PROCESS CHECK OUT APPENDIX A THROUGH I

"Current statistics indicate that African American boys represent only 9% of the total student enrollment in public schools, yet in the category of mental retardation their enrollment percentage is more than double (20%). In other categories such as emotional disturbance and learning disability, African American males are again overly represented accounting for 21% and 12% respectively."

US Department of Education NCES

APPENDIX A

THE IEP TEAM IS USUALLY MADE UP OF THE FOLLOWING:

The IEP teams is made up of individuals who bring different perspectives and expertise to the table. Combining their knowledge, team members set out to develop an individualized response to a specific child's needs, taking into account that child's strengths and talents. Each person's information adds to the team's understanding of the child and what services the child needs.

- the parents or legal guardian
- at least one of the child's special education teachers
- at least one regular education teacher
- a representative of the school system
- an individual who can interpret the evaluation results
- representatives of any other agencies that may be responsible for paying for or providing transition services (if the student is 16 years or, if appropriate, younger)
- the student, depending on age
- other individuals who have knowledge or special expertise about the child

APPENDIX B

SPECIAL EDUCATION DISABILITY CATEGORIES

IDEA lists 13 different disability categories under which 3- through 21-year-olds may be eligible for services. The disability categories listed in IDEA are:

- autism;
- deaf-blindness;
- deafness;
- emotional disturbance;
- hearing impairment;
- intellectual disability;
- multiple disabilities;
- orthopedic impairment;
- other health impairment;
- specific learning disability;
- speech or language impairment;
- traumatic brain injury; or
- visual impairment (including blindness).

IDEA further defines each of these disability terms.

For more details, definition and explanations visit www. nichcy.org

APPENDIX C

SPECIAL EDUCATION STUDENT PLACEMENT

- Inclusion education class with your peers along with a special education teacher
- Resource Room: classes with a Special Education teacher in small groups based on what subjects you need help
- Self-contained: All of your classes in same room with a Special Education teacher and usually a paraprofessional
- Separate school includes students who receive special education and related services in separate day schools for students with disabilities for more than 50 percent of the school day.
- Residential facility includes students who receive education in a public or private residential facility, at public expense, for more than 50 percent of the school day.
- Homebound/hospital environment includes students placed in and receiving special education in hospital or homebound programs.

APPENDIX D

IEP REQUIREMENTS

Annual Goals
Progress Measurement
Present Level Performance
Least Restrictive Environment
Strategies For Evaluation
Adaptations and Modifications
Description of Special Education Services
Transition Outline and Plan
Length and Duration of Services; Date (s)

Source: National Dissemination Center for Children with Disabilities, the following are the essential components of the IEP. More detail definition and explanation visit www. nichcy.org

APPENDIX E

COMMON SPECIAL EDUCATION ACRONYMS

ADA - Americans with Disabilities Act
ADD - Attention Deficit Disorder
ADHD - Attention Deficit Hypersensitivity Disorder
AYP - Adequate Yearly Progress
BD - Behavioral Disabilities
CST - Child Study Team
DOE - Department of Education
ICR - In-Class Resource with Special Ed. Teacher
IDEA - Individuals with Disabilities Education Improvement Act
IEP - Individualized Educational Plan
LDTC - Learning Disability Teacher Consultant
LRE - Least Restrictive Environment
MDT - Multidisciplinary Team
PLP - Present Level Performance
SC - Self-Contained
SI - Supplemental Instruction (taught by regular Ed. teacher)
SLD - Slow Learning Disability

APPENDIX F

SPECIAL EDUCATION IEP KEY TERMS

It is important that you become familiar with Key Terms in order to communicate with your Case Manager and other IEP Team Members.

Accommodation: This is a change to or in your child's learning environment. Accommodations can help her learn and then show what she's learned without having her challenges get in the way. For instance, if your child takes longer to answer questions, she might be allowed extra time to take a test. Even with accommodations, kids are expected to learn the same content as their peers.

Adequate Yearly Progress (AYP): Required by the No Child Left Behind Act (NCLB), all public school campuses, school districts, and the state are evaluated for AYP. Each is required to meet AYP criteria on three measures: reading/language arts, mathematics, and either graduation rate (for high schools and districts) or attendance rate (for elementary and middle/ junior high schools)

Advocate: a person who has a high degree of skill and knowledge about education and gives expert advice about this field for the purpose of supporting children.

Annual goals: The IEP document lists the academic and functional (everyday) skills the IEP team thinks your child can achieve by the end of the year. These goals are geared toward helping your child take part in the general education classroom. IEP goals need to be realistic and measurable.

Assessment: A way of collecting information about a student's special learning needs, strengths, and interests to help make educational decisions.

Assistive technology (AT): Any device, equipment or software that helps your child work around her issues. AT can help your child learn, communicate and function better in school. AT ranges from simple tools (like highlighters) to high-tech software (like apps that reads text aloud).

Autism: Autism means a developmental disability significantly affecting verbal and nonverbal communication and social interaction, generally evident before age three, that adversely affects a child's educational performance.

Behavior intervention plan (BIP): A plan designed to teach and reward positive behavior. Typically, the plan uses strategies to prevent and stop problem behaviors. It may also have supports and aids for the child. A BIP is often included as part of an IEP. To get a BIP, a child must have a functional behavioral assessment.

Case Manager: A Case Manager is a certified special educator who oversees the special education processes and verifies that IEP services are implemented in compliance with federal, state and district regulations.

Child Study Team (CST): The Child Study Team (CST) is comprised of school personnel who are trained to be specialists in the area of disability. CST members are responsible for identification, evaluation, determination of eligibility, development and review of the Individualized Education Program (IEP), and placement. Members of the CST may also deliver related services, such as school-based individual and group counseling, to students with disabilities.

Disability: A condition recognized by the law. To qualify for an IEP, your child must have a disability that is one of the 13 categories listed in the Individuals with Disabilities Education Act. Kids' learning and attention issues usually fit into one of three categories: (1) specific learning disability, (2) other health impairment (ADHD) and (3) speech or language impairment.

Due process: A formal process for resolving disputes with a school about special education and IEPs. Due process isn't the only way to resolve a dispute. There are other options, like mediation and filing a state complaint.

Eligibility: the process of qualifying for a service under one of the federally defined disability categories; a MDT meeting that considers that qualification.

Evaluation: to examine, judge, and analyze the data collected through the assessment process.

Extended school year services (ESY): Some students receive special education services outside of the regular school year, such as during the summer or, less commonly, during extended breaks like winter break.

FAPE (free appropriate public education): the guaranteed right of children with disabilities to receive an education that meets their unique needs at no cost to parents.

General education: a standard curriculum adopted by the state or local school district for all children from preschool to high school; the setting where this instruction routinely takes place.
 This is the knowledge and skills that all students throughout a state are expected to master. The curriculum varies from state to state.

Inclusion: the idea or philosophy related to students with disabilities participating and being educated in the general education classroom/program to the extent possible.

Individuals with Disabilities Education Improvement Act (IDEA): first enacted in 1975 as the Education for all Handicapped Children Act, and subsequently periodically reauthorized, it is a comprehensive federally funded law that governs the education of students with disabilities.

Individualized Education Plan (IEP): a legal document designed by a team of educators, specialists, and the child's parent(s)/guardian(s) for students eligible as described in IDEA 2004; has many required sections, specifying many aspects of a disabled child's education.

Least restrictive environment (LRE): Students with documented disabilities must be taught in the least restrictive environment. This means they must be taught in the same setting as students without documented disabilities as much as possible. The school must offer services and supports to help a child with an IEP succeed in a general education classroom.

Modification: A modification is a change in what a student is expected to learn and demonstrate. For example, a teacher might ask the class to write an essay that analyzes three major battles during a war. A child with a modification may only be asked to write about the basic facts of those battles. Modifications are different from accommodations. Parent report: This is a letter you write. It's a good way for you to document your child's strengths, struggles and success at school, at home and in the community. By sharing the report with your child's IEP team, you give them a more complete view of your child.

Progress reporting: How a school will report to you on your child's progress on annual goals. This is specified in the IEP.

Present level of performance (PLOP, PLP, PLAFF, PLAAFP): This is a snapshot of how your child is doing right now. PLOP describes your child's academic skills (such as reading level) and functional skills (such as making conversation or writing with a pencil). The school prepares this report for the IEP meeting. This is the starting point for setting annual IEP goals.

Standards-based IEP: This alternative to the traditional IEP is only used in some states. A standards-based IEP measures a student's academic performance against what the state expects of other students in the same grade.

Special education: Specially designed instruction to meet the unique needs of your child. It should be designed to give her access to the general education curriculum. The instruction is provided at no cost to you.

Supplementary aids and services: These are supports to help your child learn in the general education classroom. They can include equipment or assistive technology, like audiobooks or highlighted classroom notes. They may also include training for staff to help them work with your child.

Related services: Any support services your child needs to benefit from special education. One possible example is transportation. Another is occupational therapy.

Transition plan: This part of the IEP lays out what your teen must learn and do in high school in order to succeed as a young adult. She and the IEP team develop the plan together before it kicks in at age 16. The transition plan includes goals and activities that are academic and functional. But they extend beyond school to practical life skills and job training.

Source: https://www.understood.org/en/school-learning/special-services/ieps/iep-terms-to-know

APPENDIX G

PARENTS IEP RIGHTS

What if Your Parents Don't Agree With the IEP? The Next Steps...

For different reasons parents may not agree with the school's suggestion about your proposed IEP plan. The law allows your parents the right to challenge decisions about your eligibility, evaluation, placement, and the services that the school provides. If parents disagree with the school's actions or refusal to take action concerning certain concerns, there are several steps they may take.

- Try to reach an agreement. Parents can talk with school officials about their concerns and try to reach an agreement.
- Ask for mediation. During mediation, the parents and school sit down with someone who is not involved in the disagreement and try to reach an agreement. The school may offer mediation, if it is available as an option for resolving disputes prior to due process.
- Ask for due process. During a due process hearing, the parents and school personnel appear before an impartial hearing officer and present their sides of the story. The hearing officer decides how to solve the problem.
- File a complaint with the state education agency. To

file a complaint, generally parents write directly to the SEA and say what part of IDEA they believe the school has violated.

Center for Parents Information and Resources. Options, 1-2-3.
September 2012
A legacy resource from NICHCY
http://www.parentcenterhub.org/repository/disputes-overview/

APPENDIX H

REFERENCES

(n.d.). Retrieved September 17, 2015, from https://www.understood.org/en/learning-attention-issues/personal-stories/famous-people/success-stories-celebrities-with-dyslexia-adhd-and-dyscalculia.

(n.d.). Retrieved September 17, 2015, from http://www.socialstudieshelp.com/topics/high-school-2.html

(n.d.). Retrieved September 1, 2015, from http://www.readingrockets.org/article/iep-team-members

Archived: Guide to the Individualized Education Program. (n.d.). Retrieved August 11, 2015, from http://www2.ed.gov/parents/needs/speced/iepguide/index.html

Five Options, 1-2-3 | Center for Parent Information and Resources. (n.d.). Retrieved August 2, 2015, from http://www.parentcenterhub.org/repository/disputes-overview/

IEP's Individual Education Plans. (n.d.). Retrieved August 2, 2015, from http://specialed.about.com/od/iep/

Kids With Special Needs. (n.d.). Retrieved September

17, 2015, from http://kidshealth.org/kid/feeling/friend/special_needs.html

Lyness, A. (2014, September 1). Individualized Education Programs (IEPs). Retrieved August 9, 2015, from http://kidshealth.org/parent/growth/learning/iep.html

More, C., Hart- Barnett, J. (2014). Developing Individualized IEP Goals in the Age of Technology: Quality Challenges and Solutions.Preventing School Failure; 2014, Vol. 58 Issue 2, p103-109, 7p

New Jersey Department of Education - Special Education. (n.d.). Retrieved August 13, 2015, from http://www.state.nj.us/education/specialed/

Section 504. (n.d.). Retrieved October 1, 2015, from http://www.help4adhd.org/en/education/rights/504

Section 504 - Civil Rights Law, Protection from Discrimination - Wrightslaw. (n.d.). Retrieved October 1, 2015, from http://www.wrightslaw.com/info/sec504.index.htm

Supporting Friendship Development For Students with Low ... (n.d.). Retrieved September 29, 2015, from http://ici.umn.edu/products/impact/241/8.html

Supporting Friendship Development For Students

with Low ... (n.d.). Retrieved August 4, 2015, from http://ici.umn.edu/products/impact/241/8.html

Topic Education Center - News - May Institute. (n.d.). Retrieved August 4, 2015, from http://www.mayinstitute.org/news/topic_center.html?id=1113#sthash.v8EtYBWH.dpuf

Understanding the IEP Process. (n.d.). Retrieved October 9, 2015, from http://www.understandingspecialeducation.com/IEP-process.html

What is an IEP? | GreatKids. (n.d.). Retrieved August 2, 2015, from http://www.greatschools.org/gk/articles/what-is-an-iep/

When the IEP Team Meets | Center for Parent Information and Resources. (n.d.). Retrieved August 1, 2015, from http://www.parentcenterhub.org/repository/meetings/

Wilmshurst, L., & Brue, A. (2010). The complete guide to special education: Proven advice on evaluations, IEPs, and helping kids succeed (2nd ed.). San Francisco: Jossey-Bass.

APPENDIX I

ADDITIONAL RESOURCES

1. Log on to Especially4MePublishing.com and click the Resources tab for additional Special Education information and services.

2. See IDEA categories of Disabilities covered by Special Education laws: http://teach.com/what-is-special-education

3. The Electronic IEP

Technology is more evident in schools today. Electronic IEP programs are being implemented by many school districts as part of special education service delivery. These programs provide a useful technology that can facilitate compliance with IDEA requirements in IEP development while significantly reducing paperwork and handwritten documents.

Many school districts have adopted commercially available software or templates for electronic Individualized Education Program (IEP development. These programs have useful features that allow Individualized Education Programs to be electronically developed and reliably stored for each student. Program features are designed to enhance efficiency in the development of Individualized

Education Program goals and increase compliance with state and federal regulations.

More, C., Hart- Barnett, J. (2014). Developing **Individualized IEP** Goals in the Age of Technology: Quality Challenges and Solutions.Preventing School Failure; 2014, Vol. 58 Issue 2, p103-109, 7p

4. Your High School Years

High school provides students with the opportunity to build meaningful friendships, however, this can be a very anticipatory time for young people. It's those critical four years before entering college or the workforce. It's also a time when kids are becoming young adults, learning about friendships and relationships, and coming into their own personalities and discovering who they are. High school is perhaps the most important time in kids' lives, because they are making friendships that can last a lifetime, they're learning somewhat more advanced material, and they are preparing themselves to go out into the real world. A great help during the high school years is the teacher, case manager or guidance counselor. After school clubs, activities and sports are another very positive thing for kids to participate in. It can not only boost self esteem, but teach them how to work together as a team, an invaluable lesson for real life. The most important thing about high school is the

relationships that kids form with each other. Many people keep in touch from their high school years, and end up forming life long friendships.
High School, The Social Studies help Center. http://www.socialstudieshelp.com/topics/high-school-2.html

5. Making New Friends: Increase Social Interaction

Kids want to have friends. But it's not so easy for special needs children to find meaningful friendships with others. Some children are shy and lacks confidence because of physical differences. Others have social and communication deficits that make it difficult to start and keep friendships. Making new friends involves being in the right place at the right time. Football games, the mall, school clubs, dances, and self-advocacy groups are great places to connect with others who may have similar interests. Before approaching a new friendship, however, it's important to determine whether or not the person wants to make friends. You can do this by asking him or her directly, or by observing this person in the company of others. Smiling, gazing, and pointing are great indicators of interest and attraction.

Helping Individuals with Special Needs Develop Friendships. May Institute. Retrieved November 12, 2014 from: http://www.mayinstitute.org/news/topic_center.html?id=1113#sthash.v8EtYBWH.dpuf

ABOUT THE AUTHOR

Dr. Angelise M. Rouse is an education writer and staunch special education advocate. Her interest focus is on creating a meaningful, lasting and empowering educational experience for students with disabilities. Her research examines the development of opportunities to learn in special education classrooms, and how these opportunities are negotiated differently by various groups of students.

Inspired by her doctoral dissertation topic, Dr. Rouse future research interests are in the overrepresentation of minorities in special education and the emotional development of African American young males. Dr. Rouse holds several educational certifications and has been thoroughly published on critical educational issues. She has worked in several educational arenas serving as a charter and public school teacher, school administrator and college faculty member. Her work ranges from all levels of education from middle school through college.

Dr. Rouse holds a Ph.D. in Special Education Leadership and received a Masters in Organizational Management and Special Education. Her first book, Especially 4 Me: A Student's Guide to Understanding the IEP, was written to help promote self-advocacy for special education students. She is currently working on her next publication which will encourage and motivate young African-American males to succeed and navigate life's challenges into adulthood.

For More Information Visit

www.Especially4MePublishing.com

Or Email

contact@Especially4MePublishing.com

NOTEBOOK

NOTEBOOK

NOTEBOOK

www.ingramcontent.com/pod-product-compliance
Lightning Source LLC
Chambersburg PA
CBHW072104290426
44110CB00014B/1813